Ninja Creami
Deluxe Cookbook

The Latest & Amazing Ice Cream, Sorbet, Gelato, Milkshake, Smoothie Bowl, Lite Ice Cream, and Mix-in Recipes for Beginners

Socorro Randall

Contents

Chapter 2 Ninja Smoothie Bowls

Chapter 3 Ninja Shakes

Chapter 4 Ice Creams

Chapter 5 Ice Cream Mix-Ins

Introduction

The Ninja Creami cookbook is the ultimate choice for any food enthusiast looking to diversify their cooking repertoire. This revolutionary cookbook contains exciting new recipes, ranging from ice-creams, sorbets and milkshakes – to get you exploring outside of your culinary comfort zone. With the inclusion of unique Ninja Creami twists on traditional ingredients, you can guarantee that your taste buds will be tantalized with every bite. As a bonus, each recipe also features easy-to-follow directions - making preparing chilled drinks and ice-cream hassle-free and enjoyable. Don't miss out - unleash your culinary creativity today with the Ninja Creami cookbook!

Fundamentals of Ninja Creami

What is Ninja Creami

Ninja Creami is a revolutionary kitchen appliance that transforms frozen solid bases into delicious treats in mere seconds. It features an intuitive, one-touch operation that allows users to quickly and effortlessly create delicious homemade ice cream, sorbets, milkshakes, and more. The appliance utilizes groundbreaking technology to freeze the ingredients of your choice into creamy desserts in a matter of minutes. Simply add your preferred base – such as heavy cream, yogurt, or even vegan alternatives – and let Ninja Creami do the rest. With its powerful freezing action and state-of-the-art design, Ninja Creami makes it easy to craft unique and flavorful desserts without any mess or hassle. Plus, Ninja Creami delivers consistent results with each use so you'll never have to worry about over-frozen or under-frozen dessert bases again! Even if you're looking for a quick and tasty snack or an indulgent treat for a special occasion, Ninja Creami is the perfect solution for creating delicious decadence in minutes.

User Guide of Ninja Creami

Are you ready to make the best, most delicious ice cream of your life? If so, you're in for a treat! Introducing Ninja Creami - an innovative and revolutionary new machine that gives you the power to make restaurant quality ice cream right at home. With its easy-to-use functions and streamlined design, this beloved machine is sure to take your homemade desserts to the next level.

Filling Line

When adding ingredients to our Deluxe Pint, please be sure they don't go beyond the MAX FILL line - otherwise the ice cream can become too thick or too creamy.

Storage

Proper freezing of your ingredients is an important part of ensuring the highest quality final product. The Deluxe Pint offers a sleek and secure solution to food storage, with its tight-fitting lid that seals in freshness and prevents spills, even after a day in the deep freeze. So when your recipe calls for frozen ingredients, look no further than the Deluxe Pint – simply snap it shut and wait at least 24 hours before use!

Installation

Installing your new appliance is easy and fast! All you need to do is get your power cord, plug it into

the unit, and set it on a stable, level surface like a countertop or table. Make sure that the location of your appliance is in an area that gives good airflow, allowing the appliance to cool properly during use. Most importantly, clean off any surfaces before placing the appliance upon them - this will ensure optimal performance over time.

Thawing

Your next step in getting the most out of your Deluxe Pint is to remove the lid and place it in an outer bowl. The warmth of the bowl should cause the base to quickly thaw, giving you perfect ice cream right away, with no waiting involved.

Creamarizer Paddle

Installing the Deluxe Creamerizer™ Paddle into your outer bowl lid is a simple process! To begin, press and hold the paddle latch located at the top of the lid and slide the paddle into place. Make sure that when fully installed, the latch remains centered and you can slightly feel the paddle shake when moved. Once it's securely in place, hit the power button to get your creamerizing started!

Lock

After carefully ensuring your unit is plugged in,

it's time to get started! Locate the outer bowl onto the motor base, making sure the handle remains centered below the control panel. Once secure, give a gentle twist to the right and you'll hear a reassuring click signaling that the bowl is locked in place. You're now ready to begin using your unit with ease and efficiency.

Power

Turning on your unit is easy - simply press the power button and you'll be ready to go. The control panel will light up and you can select Top, Full, or Bottom for your program. Use the dial to find a program that matches your base, then let the unit do its work! Once complete, your program will automatically end.

Bowl Removal

When your program is done and you're ready to remove the bowl, make sure to start by grabbing the bowl release button on the left side of the motor base. Give it a gentle twist back toward its center and you should even feel the platform start to lower itself. Then, take your time with pulling it straight toward yourself until you've freed it from the motor base. After doing this, you will have successfully removed the bowl and can begin cleaning or storing it away safely.

Re-Spin Program

A crumbly or powdery Deluxe Pint can make for an unsatisfying eating experience. However, with the use of the RE-SPIN program, you can transform it into a creamy treat that isn't just enjoyable but also doubles as a piece of art! Very cold temperatures are no longer an issue either, as RE-SPIN proves to be a highly effective solution. If your treat turns out to be smooth and scoopable in consistency after all. Otherwise, put your Pint through the RE-SPIN program again and work your magic on it!

Cleanup

If your Deluxe Creamerizer™ Paddle is looking a

little worse for wear, don't worry – it's easy to clean! Just rinse the outer bowl lid to remove any sticky or liquid residue as well as pieces wedged in the paddle. Then carefully detach the paddle by pressing the latch on the top of the outer bowl lid. For easy cleanup, release paddle directly into the sink. And voila – your paddle will be good as new!

Functions

The Ninja Creami is a versatile kitchen appliance that can be used to make a vast and scrumptious variety of frozen desserts, including ice cream, sorbet, gelato, frozen yogurt, and milkshakes. With its powerful motor and sturdy construction, the Ninja Creami can handle even the most difficult tasks with ease. And cleanup is quick and breezy thanks to the removable parts that are dishwasher safe.

Here are some of the delicious recipes you can make with your Ninja Creami:

Ice Cream

Making delicious, rich, and creamy ice cream is made easier when you use a Ninja Creami. All you need to do is simply add your favorite flavors or ingredients to the machine, and let it take care of the rest. You'll have perfect ice cream in a matter of minutes! Not only is it simple to make incredible homemade ice cream with the Ninja Creami, but its precision engineering enables you to get every batch just right. So don't settle for anything less when it comes time to serve up some homemade goodness — get yourself a Ninja Creami today!

Sorbet

Making a sorbet with your Ninja Creami is the perfect way to cool down and refresh yourself! You just need to add your favorite fruit juice or puree to the machine, let it run until it's smooth, and add a bit of sugar if that's your preference. Then you can enjoy a cool and delicious treat that's sure to help beat the heat. Just think of how good that fresh sorbet will taste - it'll be

like having a little slice of summer in no time at all!

Gelato

If you're craving a rich and decadent treat, why not make your own gelato with your Ninja Creami? Add your favorite store-bought or homemade gelato mix - it's as easy as that. Then just sit back and relax while the Ninja Creami whips up something truly special. In under an hour, you'll be savoring the most flavorful, creamy gelato you've ever tasted! So why not take this chance to indulge your senses in some homemade Italian goodness? The Ninja Creami will make sure it's perfect every time.

Frozen Yogurt

If you're looking for a healthier and efficient way to satisfy your cravings for frozen desserts,

consider trying out the Ninja Creami and making homemade frozen yogurt. Just combine your favorite yogurt - either store-bought or homemade - and let the machine take care of the rest until it reaches a nice, smooth consistency. Once finished, you can customize your frozen yogurt with different fruits or other toppings if you like, then you can dig into an enjoyable treat without

any guilt! Experience a new way to enjoy frozen desserts today with the Ninja Creami.

Milkshakes

Making milkshakes with your Ninja Creami couldn't be easier! In a matter of just some

minutes, you can create perfectly blended and delicious milkshakes at just the press of a button. With your choice of ice cream mix and milk, you can quickly make any flavor milkshake that your heart desires. Making milkshakes has never been so simple and enjoyable – forget about all the mess and hassle, because Ninja Creami does it all for you! Enjoy these perfect milkshakes with family and friends for an afternoon treat like no other.

Frozen Drinks

Nothing beats a refreshing smoothie or milkshake on a hot summer day. With the Ninja Creami, you can easily make your own frozen drinks at home. Simply add your desired ingredients to the machine and it will quickly blend them into a smooth and refreshing drink. Even if you're in the mood for a fruity smoothie or a chocolate frappe, the Ninja Creami can help you make it happen. So beat the heat with your very own homemade frozen treat!

Slushies

The Ninja Creami is perfect for making slushies.

It's quick and easy to use - simply add your favorite beverage to the machine and it will quickly turn it into a refreshing slushie. Plus, it's great for making large batches so you can share with your friends.

Iced Coffee

Enjoy a delicious iced coffee in seconds with the Ninja Creami! Perfect for a hot summer's day, you can easily make the perfect cup of iced coffee to keep you cool and energized. Add cold brew coffee or espresso to the machine and watch as it quickly creates your beverage. Experiment with different amounts and ratios for your ideal flavor - using the Ninja Creami, it's easy to find your favorite recipe. Making iced coffee has never been so effortless!

Italian Ice

Italian Ice is a great way to cool off on hot summer days. With products like Ninja Creami, the task of making refreshing Italian Ice has never been simpler. You can just add water and your favorite fruity flavors of choice into the machine, and it'll quickly craft delicious dessert treats for you in no time! Enjoy creamy and cool scoops of homemade Italian ice all summer long with an easy-to-use machine like Ninja Creami.

Options/Buttons

Are you looking for a way to make your frozen dessert cravings even more special? Look no farther than the Ninja Creami machine! This

revolutionary appliance offers you unique options and buttons that let you create an amazing selection of frozen desserts unlike anything else on the market. So what are these buttons, exactly? Take a look at all that the Ninja Creami has to offer in terms of its options and buttons, so read on and discover just how many sweet treats you can make with it!

Power Button

The power button is located at the front side of the Ninja Creami unit. To turn the Ninja Creami on, press and hold the power button for some seconds. The power indicator will turn green, indicating that the unit is on. To turn the unit off, press and hold the power button for three seconds. The power indicator will turn red, indicating that the unit is off.

Install Light

When the unit is not assembled fully for use, it will illuminate. If the light is blinking, make sure that your bowl is properly installed. On the other hand, if the light remains solid, check that your paddle is properly in place. No matter what occurs, you'll be

able to quickly determine what needs to be done and get started on your project with confidence!

Countdown Timer

When it comes to getting the perfect consistency, a countdown timer can be your best friend. The Ninja Creami is no exception, featuring a convenient and user-friendly countdown timer that will help you get delicious recipes like milkshakes, ice-cream and sorbets right every time. With this exacting precision built into your recipe, you'll be free to host parties or simply enjoy the amazing culinary creations for yourself - worry free! So start tapping in those ingredients and let that countdown timer do the heavy-lifting for you.

One Touch Program

One-Touch Programs are a convenient way of making any kind of frozen dessert quickly and easily. These programs are based on intelligent designs, accurately calculating the ideal settings like speed and length ensuring perfect results each time. From ice-cream to sorbet or milkshake, these recipes can all be made in no time at all effortlessly with One-Touch Programs. So what's stopping you from tantalizing your taste buds with creamy delights today? Give it a go and let One-Touch Programs do all the hard work!

Cleaning of Ninja Creami is essential to keep your ice cream maker in top condition. Not only will it ensure that your machine works properly, but it will also help to prevent any cross contamination of flavors.

Before cleaning the Ninja Creami, unplug the machine from the power outlet.

Use a damp cloth to thoroughly wipe down the

exterior of the machine. Be sure to avoid getting water on or near the electrical components.

To clean the freezing bowl, remove it from the machine and hand wash it with warm, soapy water. Rinse thoroughly and dry before returning it to the Creami.

The paddles can be removed for cleaning by unscrewing them from the shaft. Wash them in warm, soapy water and rinse before returning them to the machine.

To clean the interior of the Creami, use a soft-bristled brush or sponge to wipe away any buildup of ice cream or other frozen products.

Once you have cleaned all of the removable parts, wipe down the inside of the machine with a damp cloth. Again, take great care to avoid getting water on or near any electrical components.

Finally, dry all of the parts thoroughly before plugging the machine back in and using it again.

It's true that Ninja Creami requires a bit of extra care and maintenance, but the effort is well worth it in order to keep your appliance looking its best. From regular cleanings to avoiding wear-and-tear activities, there are few steps you can take to make sure your beloved Ninja Creami always looks as new as ever.

Unplugging the Ninja™ CREAMi®

Before starting any maintenance work on the Ninja™ CREAMi®, be sure to unplug it from the power outlet.

Cleaning the Exterior

Use a damp cloth to wipe down the outside of the machine to remove any dust particles and dirt that has built up over time.

Checking Machine Components

Inspect all components of the machine, such as paddles, and other parts, for signs of wear or damage. Make sure they are properly secured in place and that all screws are tight.

Sanitizing

Wipe down all surfaces with a mild sanitizing solution and a clean cloth. Be sure to allow the sanitizing solution to sit for a few minutes for more effective results before wiping it off.

Checking for Unusual Sounds

Listen closely for any unusual noises coming from within the machine while it's running. If you hear anything out of the ordinary, turn off the machine immediately and contact customer service for assistance in diagnosing and fixing any issues you may have found.

Lubricating Moving Parts

Apply light lubricants such as vegetable oil or silicon spray to areas with moving parts such as bearings or hinges in order to reduce friction and ensure smooth operation of your Ninja™ Creami® machine over time.

Testing Operation

Once all maintenance tasks have been completed and you've checked everything is working correctly, you can test run your machine before using it again by adding some frozen solid base into one of its containers and pressing start button to see if it works correctly and produces ice cream, sorbets, milkshakes, etc., as expected.

Benefits of Using It

The Ninja Creami comes with a wide array of benefits that make it easy to enjoy delicious treats in the comfort of your own home.

The Ninja™ CREAMi® can quickly and easily turn frozen solid bases into delicious ice cream, sorbets, milkshakes, and more.

With the touch of a single button, you can have your favorite frozen treats in no time.

The Ninja™ CREAMi® is perfect for those who love ice cream, sorbet, or milkshake but don't want to spend hours making it themselves.

The Ninja™ CREAMi® is also great for those who want to experiment with different flavors and ingredients to create their own unique frozen treats.

With the Ninja™ CREAMi®, you can make ice cream, sorbet, or milkshake that is low in fat, calories, and sugar but still tastes great.

The Ninja™ CREAMi® is also very easy to clean, so you can enjoy your frozen treats without worry. The Ninja™ CREAMi® is an essential kitchen appliance for anyone who loves ice cream, sorbet, or milkshake!

Enhance Your Ice-Cream Makins Skills. Ninja Creami is a revolutionary frozen dessert maker that brings a professional-level of convenience, quality and creativity to all your homemade ice cream creations. With its sleek design and powerful features, this machine makes the entire ice cream making process easy and hassle-free. It boasts simple, 1-touch operation to create gourmet soft serve or hardening full-bodied artisanal ice cream in as little as 20 minutes. Crafted with durable professional components, Ninja Creami lets you effortlessly customize your own creamy creations by mixing and matching recipes or ingredients with liquid nitrogen for a smooth texture, creative flavors, and unique magnitudes of coldness. Allow yourself to enhance your ice-cream making skills and explore infinite possibilities with Ninja Creami today.

Chapter 1 Ninja CREAMi Sorbet

Mix Fruit Sorbet

Preparation Time: 5 minutes | Servings: 2

Ingredients:

¾ cup ripe pineapple, cut into ½-inch pieces   1¼ mangoes, peeled, cut into ½-inch pieces

1 ripe banana, cut into ½-inch slices

Preparation:

1. In a Ninja CREAMi pint, move the mangoes along with the pineapples and bananas, and fasten the container with a lid. 2. Freeze the pint for 24 hours. 3. After 24 hours, open the pint, fix it into the outer bowl of Ninja CREAMi, along with the 'Creamerizer paddle'. 4. Fasten the lid, turn on the unit, and select the 'SORBET' function. 5. Dish out the sorbet from the pint and serve chilled.

Nutritional Information per Serving:

Calories: 203 | Fat: 0.6g | Sat Fat: 0.2g | Carbohydrates: 52g | Fiber: 7.6g | Sugar: 34g | Protein: 3g

Smooth Banana Sorbet

Preparation Time: 5 minutes | Cooking Time: 3minutes | Servings: 4

Ingredients:

4 large bananas   Water, as required

Preparation:

1. In a blender, blitz all the ingredients until smooth. 2. In a Ninja CREAMi pint, move the mixture and fasten the container with a lid. 3. Freeze the pint for 24 hours. 4. After 24 hours, open the pint, fix it into the outer bowl of Ninja CREAMi along with the 'Creamerizer paddle'. 5. Fasten the lid, turn on the 'Power Button', and select the 'SORBET' function. 6. Dish out the sorbet from the pint and serve chilled.

Nutritional Information per Serving:

Calories: 61 | Fat: 0.2g | Sat Fat: 0.1g | Carbohydrates: 15.5g | Fiber: 1.8g | Sugar: 8.3g | Protein: 0.7g

Sweet Apricot Sorbet

Preparation Time: 40 minutes | Servings: 8

Ingredients:

2 tablespoons lemon juice, freshly squeezed

2 cups apricots, chopped and pitted

1 cup hot water

1 cup sugar, granulated

Preparation:

1. Blitz apricots with all other ingredients in a blender until smooth. 2. In a Ninja CREAMi pint, move the mixture and fasten the container with a lid. 3. Freeze the pint for 24 hours. 4. After 24 hours, open the pint, fix it into the outer bowl of Ninja CREAMi along with the 'Creamerizer paddle'. 5. Fasten the lid, turn on the 'Power Button', and select the 'SORBET' function. 6. Dish out the sorbet from the pint and serve chilled.

Nutritional Information per Serving:

Calories: 116 | Fat: 1g | Sat Fat: 1g | Carbohydrates: 30g | Fiber: 1g | Sugar: 29g | Protein: 1g

Persimmon Sorbet

Preparation Time: 10 minutes | Servings: 4

Ingredients:

1¾-liter ice cream, softened

2 cups persimmon pulp

½ can condensed milk, sweetened

Preparation:

1. In a bowl, merge the persimmon pulp with condensed milk and ice cream. 2. In a Ninja CREAMi pint, move the mixture and fasten the container with a lid. 3. Freeze the pint for 24 hours. 4. After 24 hours, open the pint, fix it into the outer bowl of Ninja CREAMi along with the 'Creamerizer paddle'. 5. Fasten the lid, turn on the 'Power Button', and select the 'SORBET' function. 6. Dish out the sorbet from the pint and serve chilled.

Nutritional Information per Serving:

Calories: 183 | Fat: 6g | Sat Fat: 4g | Carbohydrates: 27g | Fiber: 0.2g | Sugar: 26g | Protein: 4g

Pomegranate and Cherry Sorbet

Preparation Time: 15 minutes | Servings: 3

Ingredients:

½ cup pomegranate juice   1 can cherries

Preparation:

1. In a Ninja CREAMi pint, move the cherries and juice and fasten the container with a lid. 2. Freeze the pint for 24 hours. 3. After 24 hours, open the pint, fix it into the outer bowl of Ninja CREAMi, along with the 'Creamerizer paddle.' 4. Fasten the lid, turn on the unit, and select the 'SORBET' function. 5. Dish out the sorbet from the pint and serve chilled.

Nutritional Information per Serving:

Calories: 110 | Fat: 0.5g | Sat Fat: 0g | Carbohydrates: 28g | Fiber: 2.8g | Sugar: 23g | Protein: 1.2g

Pineapple Basil Sorbet

Preparation Time: 10 minutes | Servings: 6

Ingredients:

1 lemon juice

1 small piece of ginger, sliced

1 can pineapple chunks

1 lemon zest

1 teaspoon basil leaves

⅓ cup sugar

Preparation:

1. In a blender, blitz all the ingredients until smooth. 2. In a Ninja CREAMi pint, move the mixture and fasten the container with a lid. 3. Freeze the pint for 24 hours. 4. After 24 hours, open the pint, fix it into the outer bowl of Ninja CREAMi along with the 'Creamerizer paddle'. 5. Fasten the lid, turn on the 'Power Button', and select the 'SORBET' function. 6. Dish out the sorbet from the pint and serve chilled.

Nutritional Information per Serving:

Calories: 34 | Fat: 0.1g | Sat Fat: 0g | Carbohydrates: 8.9g | Fiber: 0.5g | Sugar: 5.9g | Protein: 0.1g

Tasty Plum Sorbet

Preparation Time: 40 minutes | Servings: 4

Ingredients:

1 (20-ounce) can plums

Preparation:

1. In a Ninja CREAMi pint, move the plums and fasten the container with a lid. 2. Freeze the pint for 24 hours. 3. After 24 hours, open the pint, fix it into the outer bowl of Ninja CREAMi, along with the 'Creamerizer paddle'. 4. Fasten the lid, turn on the unit, and select the 'SORBET' function. 5. Dish out the sorbet from the pint and serve chilled.

Nutritional Information per Serving:

Calories: 150 | Fat: 1g | Sat Fat: 0g | Carbohydrates: 40g | Fiber: 4.5g | Sugar: 35g | Protein: 2.5g

Mixed Berry Sorbet

Preparation Time: 10 minutes | Servings: 4

Ingredients:

1 cup blueberries

1 cup raspberries

1 cup strawberries, stemmed and quartered

Preparation:

1. In a Ninja CREAMi pint, move all the berries and fasten the container with a lid. 2. Freeze the pint for 24 hours. 3. After 24 hours, open the pint, fix it into the outer bowl of Ninja CREAMi, along with the 'Creamerizer paddle'. 4. Fasten the lid, turn on the unit, and select the 'SORBET' function. 5. Dish out the sorbet from the pint and serve chilled.

Nutritional Information per Serving:

Calories: 48 | Fat: 0.4g | Sat Fat: 0g | Carbohydrates: 11g | Fiber: 3.6g | Sugar: 6.7g | Protein: 0.9g

Banana and Strawberry Sorbet

Preparation Time: 5 minutes | Servings: 4

Ingredients:

1 lb. strawberry-banana frozen fruit

⅓ cup agave nectar

3 tablespoons fresh lemon juice

Preparation:

1. In a blender, blitz all the ingredients until smooth. 2. In a Ninja CREAMi pint, move the mixture and fasten the container with a lid. 3. Freeze the pint for 24 hours. 4. After 24 hours, open the pint, fix it into the outer bowl of Ninja CREAMi along with the 'Creamerizer paddle'. 5. Fasten the lid, turn on the 'Power Button', and select the 'SORBET' function. 6. Dish out the sorbet from the pint and serve chilled.

Nutritional Information per Serving:

Calories: 122 | Fat: 0.2g | Sat Fat: 0g | Carbohydrates: 32g | Fiber: 2g | Sugar: 25g | Protein: 1g

Vanilla Rhubarb Sorbet

Preparation Time: 10 minutes | Servings: 6

Ingredients:

3 cups rhubarb, chopped

3 drops vanilla essence

3 tablespoons liquid glucose

1 lemon juice

⅔ cup golden caster sugar

2 teaspoons star anise

Preparation:

1. In a blender, blitz all the ingredients until smooth. 2. In a Ninja CREAMi pint, move the mixture and fasten the container with a lid. 3. Freeze the pint for 24 hours. 4. After 24 hours, open the pint, fix it into the outer bowl of Ninja CREAMi along with the 'Creamerizer paddle'. 5. Fasten the lid, turn on the 'Power Button', and select the 'SORBET' function. 6. Dish out the sorbet from the pint and serve chilled.

Nutritional Information per Serving:

Calories: 17 | Fat: 0.2g | Sat Fat: 0g | Carbohydrates: 3.6g | Fiber: 1.2g | Sugar: 1.1g | Protein: 0.7g

Grape Sorbet

Preparation Time: 10 minutes | Servings: 4

Ingredients:

1½ cups water

¾ cup grape juice concentrate, frozen

1 tablespoon lemon juice

Preparation:

1. In a bowl, merge the grape juice concentrate with lemon juice and water. 2. In a Ninja CREAMi pint, move the mixture and fasten the container with a lid. 3. Freeze the pint for 24 hours. 4. After 24 hours, open the pint, fix it into the outer bowl of Ninja CREAMi along with the 'Creamerizer paddle'. 5. Fasten the lid, turn on the 'Power Button', and select the 'SORBET' function. 6. Dish out the sorbet from the pint and serve chilled.

Nutritional Information per Serving:

Calories: 25 | Fat: 0.1g | Sat Fat: 0g | Carbohydrates: 6g | Fiber: 0.1g | Sugar: 6g | Protein: 0.1g

Lemony Dill and Basil Sorbet

Preparation Time: 15 minutes | Cooking Time: 6 minutes | Servings: 4

Ingredients:

½ cup water

¼ cup granulated sugar

2 large fresh dill sprigs, stemmed

2 large fresh basil sprigs, stemmed

1 cup ice water

2 tablespoons fresh lemon juice

Preparation:

1. In a saucepan, merge together sugar and water. 2. Let the sugar get dissolved over medium heat for about 5 minutes. 3. Stir in the dill and basil sprigs and eliminate from the heat. 4. Add ice water and lemon juice and mix well. 5. In a Ninja CREAMi pint, move the mixture and fasten the container with a lid. 6. Freeze the pint for 24 hours. 7. After 24 hours, open the pint, fix it into the outer bowl of Ninja CREAMi along with the 'Creamerizer paddle'. 8. Fasten the lid, turn on the 'Power Button', and select the 'SORBET' function. 9. Dish out the sorbet from the pint and serve chilled.

Nutritional Information per Serving:

Calories: 51 | Fat: 0.1g | Sat Fat: 0g.1 | Carbohydrates: 13.1g | Fiber: 0.1g | Sugar: 12.7g | Protein: 0.2g

Vanilla Coffee and Banana Sorbet

Preparation Time: 5 minutes | Servings: 2

Ingredients:

¾ cup banana, slices

⅜ cup vanilla coffee creamer

½ teaspoon vanilla extract

Preparation:

1. In a blender, blitz all the ingredients until smooth. 2. In a Ninja CREAMi pint, move the mixture and fasten the container with a lid. 3. Freeze the pint for 24 hours. 4. After 24 hours, open the pint, fix it into the outer bowl of Ninja CREAMi along with the 'Creamerizer paddle'. 5. Fasten the lid, turn on the 'Power Button', and select the 'SORBET' function. 6. Dish out the sorbet from the pint and serve chilled.

Nutritional Information per Serving:

Calories: 119 | Fat: 3g | Sat Fat: 0g | Carbohydrates: 24g | Fiber: 0.7g | Sugar: 22.6g | Protein: 0.3g

Chapter 2 Ninja Smoothie Bowls

Fruity Coconut Smoothie Bowl

Preparation Time: 10 minutes | Servings: 2

Ingredients:

1 cup coconut milk

½ cup berries, frozen

2 bananas, frozen

2 tablespoons sugar

Preparation:

1. Put all the ingredients into the MAX FILL line of a CREAMi pint. 2. Fasten the lid of the pint and freeze for 24 hours. 3. After 24 hours, open the pint, fix it into the outer bowl of Ninja CREAMi along with the 'Creamerizer paddle'. 4. Fasten the lid, turn on the 'Power Button', and select the 'SMOOTHIE BOWL' function. 5. Dish out the smoothie from the pint and serve as desired.

Nutritional Information per Serving:

Calories: 278 | Fat: 24g | Sat Fat: 21g | Carbohydrates: 7g | Fiber: 3g | Sugar: 4.3g | Protein: 2.3g

Oats and Banana Smoothie Bowl

Preparation Time: 10 minutes | Cooking Time: 0 minute | Servings: 1

Ingredients:

½ cup carrots, frozen

1 frozen banana, quartered

½ teaspoon cinnamon

¼ cup rolled oats

2 tablespoons vanilla Greek yogurt

Preparation:

1. Put the frozen carrots to the MAX FILL line of a CREAMi pint. 2. In a large bowl, merge together rolled oats, banana, vanilla Greek yogurt, and cinnamon. 3. Thoroughly blend and move the mixture in the CREAMi pint. 4. Fasten the lid of the pint and freeze for 24 hours. 5. After 24 hours, open the pint, fix it into the outer bowl of Ninja CREAMi along with the 'Creamerizer paddle'. 6. Fasten the lid, turn on the 'Power Button', and select the 'SMOOTHIE BOWL" function. 7. Dish out the smoothie from the pint and serve as desired.

Nutritional Information per Serving:

Calories: 105 | Fat: 0.9g | Sat Fat: 0.2g | Carbohydrates: 22g | Fiber: 3g | Sugar: 8g | Protein: 2g

Oat Banana Smoothie Bowl

Preparation Time: 10 minutes | Cooking Time: 1 minute | Servings: 2

Ingredients:

¼ cup quick oats

½ cup water

1 cup vanilla Greek yogurt

3 tablespoons honey

½ cup banana, peeled and sliced

Preparation:

1. Merge the water and oats and microwave for 1 minute on High. 2. Add the yogurt, banana and honey after removing from the microwave until well combined. 3. Move this mixture to the MAX FILL line of a CREAMi pint. 4. Fasten the lid of the pint and freeze for 24 hours. 5. After 24 hours, open the pint, fix it into the outer bowl of Ninja CREAMi along with the 'Creamerizer paddle'. 6. Fasten the lid, turn on the 'Power Button', and select the 'SMOOTHIE BOWL' function. 7. Dish out the smoothie from the pint and serve as desired.

Nutritional Information per Serving:

Calories: 278 | Fat: 2.7g | Sat Fat: 1.1g | Carbohydrates: 55.7g | Fiber: 2.1g | Sugar: 41.6g | Protein: 10.9g

Peaches Smoothie Bowl

Preparation Time: 10 minutes | Servings: 1

Ingredients:

1 cup almond milk, unsweetened

1 cup ice

1 scoop vanilla protein

½ cup peaches, frozen

1 tablespoon chia seeds

Preparation:

1. In a blender, blitz all the ingredients until smooth. 2. Move this mixture to the MAX FILL line of a CREAMi pint. 3. Fasten the lid of the pint and freeze for 24 hours. 4. After 24 hours, open the pint, fix it into the outer bowl of Ninja CREAMi along with the 'Creamerizer paddle'. 5. Fasten the lid, turn on the 'Power Button', and select the 'SMOOTHIE BOWL' function. 6. Dish out the smoothie from the pint and serve as desired.

Nutritional Information per Serving:

Calories: 490 | Fat: 37g | Sat Fat: 30g | Carbohydrates: 21g | Fiber: 6g | Sugar: 15g | Protein: 5g

Berries Smoothie Bowl

Preparation Time: 5 minutes | Servings: 1

Ingredients:

2 cups frozen berries

½ cup grapefruit juice

1 tablespoon sugar

Preparation:

1. In a large bowl, merge together the berries, grapefruit juice, and sugar. 2. Move this mixture to the MAX FILL line of a CREAMi pint. 3. Fasten the lid of the pint and freeze for 24 hours. 4. After 24 hours, open the pint, fix it into the outer bowl of Ninja CREAMi along with the 'Creamerizer paddle'. 5. Fasten the lid, turn on the 'Power Button', and select the 'SMOOTHIE BOWL' function. 6. Dish out the smoothie from the pint and serve as desired.

Nutritional Information per Serving:

Calories: 102 | Fat: 0.1g | Sat Fat: 0g | Carbohydrates: 30g | Fiber: 5g | Sugar: 22g | Protein: 1.2g

Refreshing Strawberry Banana Smoothie Bowl

Preparation Time: 10 minutes | Cooking Time: 0 minute | Servings: 4

Ingredients:

1 cup fresh ripe banana, sliced

2 tablespoons vanilla protein powder

¼ cup whole milk

1 cup ripe strawberries, trimmed, sliced

¼ cup raw agave nectar

¼ pineapple juice

Preparation:

1. In a large bowl, merge together the banana with all other ingredients. 2. Move this mixture to the MAX FILL line of a CREAMi pint. 3. Fasten the lid of the pint and freeze for 24 hours. 4. After 24 hours, open the pint, fix it into the outer bowl of Ninja CREAMi along with the 'Creamerizer paddle'. 5. Fasten the lid, turn on the 'Power Button', and select the 'SMOOTHIE BOWL' function. 6. Dish out the smoothie from the pint and serve as desired.

Nutritional Information per Serving:

Calories: 115 | Fat: 0.7g | Sat Fat: 0.3g | Carbohydrates: 24g | Fiber: 1g | Sugar: 23g | Protein: 1g

Coffee-flavored Raspberry Smoothie Bowl

Preparation Time: 10 minutes | Servings: 4

Ingredients:

1 cup brewed coffee

2 tablespoons almond butter

1 large banana, peeled and sliced

½ cup oat milk

1 cup fresh raspberries

Preparation:

1. In a blender, blitz all the ingredients until smooth. 2. Move this mixture to the MAX FILL line of a CREAMi pint. 3. Fasten the lid of the pint and freeze for 24 hours. 4. After 24 hours, open the pint, fix it into the outer bowl of Ninja CREAMi along with the 'Creamerizer paddle'. 5. Fasten the lid, turn on the 'Power Button', and select the 'SMOOTHIE BOWL' function. 6. Dish out the smoothie from the pint and serve as desired.

Nutritional Information per Serving:

Calories: 108 | Fat: 5.1g | Sat Fat: 0.4g | Carbohydrates: 14.9g | Fiber: 3.8g | Sugar: 7.7g | Protein: 3g

Fruity Ginger Smoothie Bowl

Preparation Time: 10 minutes | Servings: 1

Ingredients:

1 ripe banana

1 teaspoon fresh ginger, minced

½ teaspoon vanilla extract

1 cup strawberries

½ teaspoon cinnamon

½ cup almond milk, unsweetened

Preparation:

1. In a blender, blitz all the ingredients until smooth. 2. Move this mixture to the MAX FILL line of a CREAMi pint. 3. Fasten the lid of the pint and freeze for 24 hours. 4. After 24 hours, open the pint, fix it into the outer bowl of Ninja CREAMi along with the 'Creamerizer paddle'. 5. Fasten the lid, turn on the 'Power Button', and select the 'SMOOTHIE BOWL' function. 6. Dish out the smoothie from the pint and serve as desired.

Nutritional Information per Serving:

Calories: 396 | Fat: 13g | Sat Fat: 2g | Carbohydrates: 69g | Fiber: 15g | Sugar: 37g | Protein: 8g

Coconut Berries Smoothie Bowl

Preparation Time: 5 minutes | Servings: 2

Ingredients:

1 cup frozen berries

⅛ cup frozen strawberries, sliced

⅛ cup pineapple juice

⅛ cup raw agave nectar

⅛ cup coconut milk, unsweetened

Preparation:

1. In a blender, blitz all the ingredients until smooth. 2. Move this mixture to the MAX FILL line of a CREAMi pint. 3. Fasten the lid of the pint and freeze for 24 hours. 4. After 24 hours, open the pint, fix it into the outer bowl of Ninja CREAMi along with the 'Creamerizer paddle'. 5. Fasten the lid, turn on the 'Power Button', and select the 'SMOOTHIE BOWL' function. 6. Dish out the smoothie from the pint and serve as desired.

Nutritional Information per Serving:

Calories: 74 | Fat: 3g | Sat Fat: 3.2g | Carbohydrates: 10g | Fiber: 1.2g | Sugar: 8g | Protein: 0.6g

Flavorful Avocado Kale Smoothie Bowl

Preparation Time: 10 minutes | Servings: 4

Ingredients:

½ avocado, sliced

1 cup kale leaves, packed

1 cup green apples, sliced

1 banana, sliced

¼ cup coconut milk, unsweetened

2 tablespoons agave nectar

Preparation:

1. In a large bowl, merge together all the ingredients. 2. Move this mixture to the MAX FILL line of a CREAMi pint. 3. Fasten the lid of the pint and freeze for 24 hours. 4. After 24 hours, open the pint, fix it into the outer bowl of Ninja CREAMi along with the 'Creamerizer paddle'. 5. Fasten the lid, turn on the 'Power Button', and select the 'SMOOTHIE BOWL' function. 6. Dish out the smoothie from the pint and serve as desired.

Nutritional Information per Serving:

Calories: 150 | Fat: 8g | Sat Fat: 4g | Carbohydrates: 19g | Fiber: 4g | Sugar: 10g | Protein: 1g

Cranberry and Cherry Smoothie Bowl

Preparation Time: 10 minutes | Servings: 4

Ingredients:

1 cup cranberry juice cocktail

2 cups cherry berry blend, frozen

¼ cup agave nectar

Preparation:

1. In a large bowl, merge together the agave nectar and cranberry juice cocktail. 2. Put the cherry berry blend to the MAX FILL line of a CREAMi pint and top with the cocktail mixture. 3. Fasten the lid of the pint and freeze for 24 hours. 4. After 24 hours, open the pint, fix it into the outer bowl of Ninja CREAMi along with the 'Creamerizer paddle'. 5. Fasten the lid, turn on the 'Power Button', and select the 'SMOOTHIE BOWL' function. 6. Dish out the smoothie from the pint and serve as desired.

Nutritional Information per Serving:

Calories: 127 | Fat: 0.3g | Sat Fat: 0g | Carbohydrates: 1.5g | Fiber: 2.5g | Sugar: 27.5g | Protein: 0.5g

Creamy Mango Banana Smoothie Bowl

Preparation Time: 10 minutes | Servings: 2

Ingredients:

1 cup banana, frozen

3 cups mango, frozen

½ cup almond milk

2 tablespoons maple syrup

For Topping:

4 tablespoons granola

2 tablespoons passion fruit seeds

Preparation:

1. In a blender, blitz all the ingredients except for topping until smooth. 2. Move this mixture to the MAX FILL line of a CREAMi pint. 3. Fasten the lid of the pint and freeze for 24 hours. 4. After 24 hours, open the pint, fix it into the outer bowl of Ninja CREAMi along with the 'Creamerizer paddle'. 5. Fasten the lid, turn on the 'Power Button', and select the 'SMOOTHIE BOWL' function. 6. Dish out the smoothie from the pint and serve as desired.

Nutritional Information per Serving:

Calories: 423 | Fat: 7g | Sat Fat: 2g | Carbohydrates: 94g | Fiber: 11g | Sugar: 6g | Protein: 6g

Pineapple and Banana Smoothie Bowl

Preparation Time: 10 minutes | Servings: 4

Ingredients:

1 cup fresh pineapple, chopped

2 ripe bananas, peeled and cut into 1-inch pieces

¼ cup yogurt

2 tablespoons honey

Preparation:

1. In a large bowl, merge together all the ingredients. 2. Move this mixture to the MAX FILL line of a CREAMi pint. 3. Fasten the lid of the pint and freeze for 24 hours. 4. After 24 hours, open the pint, fix it into the outer bowl of Ninja CREAMi along with the 'Creamerizer paddle'. 5. Fasten the lid, turn on the 'Power Button', and select the 'SMOOTHIE BOWL' function. 6. Dish out the smoothie from the pint and serve as desired.

Nutritional Information per Serving:

Calories: 116 | Fat: 0.4g | Sat Fat: 0.2g | Carbohydrates: 28.6g | Fiber: 2.1g | Sugar: 21g | Protein: 1.8g

Chapter 3 Ninja Shakes

Hazelnut Milkshake

Preparation Time: 5 minutes | Servings: 2

Ingredients:

1½ cups hazelnut ice cream

½ cup whole milk

¼ cup chocolate spread

Preparation:

1. Move all the ingredients into a CREAMi pint container and merge well. 2. Fasten the lid of the pint and freeze for 24 hours. 3. After 24 hours, open the pint, fix it into the outer bowl of Ninja CREAMi along with the 'Creamerizer paddle'. 4. Fasten the lid, turn on the 'Power Button', and select the 'MILKSHAKE' function. 5. Ladle out the shake into serving glasses and serve chilled.

Nutritional Information per Serving:

Calories: 209 | Fat: 11g | Sat Fat: 5g | Carbohydrates: 21g | Fiber: 0.8g | Sugar: 20g | Protein: 4g

Vegan Chocolate Banana Milkshake

Preparation Time: 2 minutes | Cooking Time: 0 minute | Servings: 2

Ingredients:

½ cup cashew milk

1½ cups vegan chocolate ice cream

½ cup fresh banana, ripe

1 tablespoon coffee powder, instant

Preparation:

1. Move the ice cream into a CREAMi pint container. 2. Use a spoon to make a hole that is 1½ inches wide in the pint's bottom. 3. Add the remaining ingredients to the hole. 4. Fasten the lid of the pint and freeze for 24 hours. 5. After 24 hours, open the pint, fix it into the outer bowl of Ninja CREAMi along with the 'Creamerizer paddle'. 6. Fasten the lid, turn on the 'Power Button', and select the 'MILKSHAKE' function. 7. Ladle out the shake into serving glasses and serve chilled.

Nutritional Information per Serving:

Calories: 142 | Fat: 5.9g | Sat Fat: 3.4g | Carbohydrates: 20g | Fiber: 1g | Sugar: 15g | Protein: 2g

Marshmallow Oat Milkshake

Preparation Time: 10 minutes | Servings: 2

Ingredients:

1½ cups vanilla ice cream

½ cup oat milk

½ cup marshmallow cereal

Preparation:

1. Move the ice cream, oat milk, and marshmallow cereal into a CREAMi pint container. 2. Fasten the lid of the pint and freeze for 24 hours. 3. After 24 hours, open the pint, fix it into the outer bowl of Ninja CREAMi along with the 'Creamerizer paddle'. 4. Fasten the lid, turn on the 'Power Button', and select the 'MILKSHAKE' function. 5. Ladle out the shake into serving glasses and serve chilled.

Nutritional Information per Serving:

Calories: 165 | Fat: 6.1g | Sat Fat: 3.5g | Carbohydrates: 24.8g | Fiber: 1.1g | Sugar: 19.3g | Protein: 3g

Pumpkin Latte Milkshake

Preparation Time: 5 minutes | Servings: 4

Ingredients:

2 cups whole milk

2 tablespoons sugar, granulated

1 cup coffee, brewed

4 cups vanilla ice cream

½ cup pumpkin puree, canned

1 teaspoon pumpkin pie spice

2 teaspoons vanilla extract

1 cup ice cubes

Preparation:

1. In a saucepan, lightly boil the milk and then ladle out in a mixing bowl. 2. Merge in the pumpkin, sugar, pumpkin pie spice, coffee, and vanilla essence. 3. Whisk well and refrigerate for an hour. 4. Move the mixture into a CREAMi pint container along with vanilla ice cream. 5. Fasten the lid of the pint and freeze for 24 hours. 6. After 24 hours, open the pint, fix it into the outer bowl of Ninja CREAMi along with the 'Creamerizer paddle'. 7. Fasten the lid, turn on the 'Power Button', and select the 'MILKSHAKE' function. 8. Ladle out the shake into serving glasses and serve chilled.

Nutritional Information per Serving:

Calories: 260 | Fat: 11g | Sat Fat: 6g | Carbohydrates: 30g | Fiber: 1g | Sugar:27 g | Protein: 6 g

Cashew Chocolate Milkshake

Preparation Time: 5 minutes | Servings: 2

Ingredients:

½ cup cashew milk

1½ cups chocolate ice cream

½ cup ripe banana, cut into pieces

1 tablespoon instant coffee powder

Preparation:

1. Move all the ingredients into a CREAMi pint container except the chocolate chip cookies. 2. Fasten the lid of the pint and freeze for 24 hours. 3. After 24 hours, open the pint, fix it into the outer bowl of Ninja CREAMi along with the 'Creamerizer paddle'. 4. Fasten the lid, turn on the 'Power Button', and select the 'MILKSHAKE' function. 5. Ladle out the shake into serving glasses and serve chilled.

Nutritional Information per Serving:

Calories: 269 | Fat: 12g | Sat Fat: 7.7g | Carbohydrates: 40g | Fiber: 2.4g | Sugar: 32g | Protein: 4g

Rainbow Vanilla Cake Milkshake

Preparation Time: 2 minutes | Servings: 2

Ingredients:

2 cups vegan French vanilla coffee creamer

1 tablespoon raw agave nectar

2-ounces vanilla vodka

1 tablespoon rainbow sprinkles

Preparation:

1. Move all the ingredients into a CREAMi pint container except the chocolate chip cookies. 2. Fasten the lid of the pint and freeze for 24 hours. 3. After 24 hours, open the pint, fix it into the outer bowl of Ninja CREAMi along with the 'Creamerizer paddle'. 4. Fasten the lid, turn on the 'Power Button', and select the 'MILKSHAKE' function. 5. Ladle out the shake into serving glasses and serve chilled.

Nutritional Information per Serving:

Calories: 541 | Fat: 34g | Sat Fat: 18g | Carbohydrates: 6g | Fiber: 0g | Sugar: 2g | Protein: 5g

Vanilla Pecan Milkshake

Preparation Time: 10 minutes | Servings: 2

Ingredients:

1½ cups vanilla ice cream

2 tablespoons maple syrup

¼ cup pecans, chopped

Pinch of salt

½ cup soy milk, unsweetened

1 teaspoon ground cinnamon

Preparation:

1. Move the ice cream, soy milk, maple syrup, pecans, cinnamon and salt into a CREAMi pint container. 2. Fasten the lid of the pint and freeze for 24 hours. 3. After 24 hours, open the pint, fix it into the outer bowl of Ninja CREAMi along with the 'Creamerizer paddle'. 4. Fasten the lid, turn on the 'Power Button', and select the 'MILKSHAKE' function. 5. Ladle out the shake into serving glasses and serve chilled.

Nutritional Information per Serving:

Calories: 309 | Fat: 18.5g | Sat Fat: 4.7g | Carbohydrates: 32.6g | Fiber: 3.2g | Sugar: 25.5g | Protein: 5.6g

Creamy Praline Milkshake

Preparation Time: 5 minutes | Servings: 2

Ingredients:

3 cups praline ice cream

1 cup milk

1½ ounces whiskey

Preparation:

1. Move all the ingredients into a CREAMi pint container. 2. Fasten the lid of the pint and freeze for 24 hours. 3. After 24 hours, open the pint, fix it into the outer bowl of Ninja CREAMi along with the 'Creamerizer paddle'. 4. Fasten the lid, turn on the 'Power Button', and select the 'MILKSHAKE' function. 5. Ladle out the shake into serving glasses and serve chilled.

Nutritional Information per Serving:

Calories: 320 | Fat: 13g | Sat Fat: 8g | Carbohydrates: 30g | Fiber: 0g | Sugar: 26g | Protein: 7g

Refreshing Mint Cookie Milkshake

Preparation Time: 5 minutes | Servings: 4

Ingredients:

3 cream cookies

¼ cup milk

1½ cups mint ice cream

Preparation:

1. Move all the ingredients into a CREAMi pint container. 2. Fasten the lid of the pint and freeze for 24 hours. 3. After 24 hours, open the pint, fix it into the outer bowl of Ninja CREAMi along with the 'Creamerizer paddle'. 4. Fasten the lid, turn on the 'Power Button', and select the 'MILKSHAKE' function. 5. Ladle out the shake into serving glasses and serve chilled.

Nutritional Information per Serving:

Calories: 113 | Fat: 2g | Sat Fat: 0.8g | Carbohydrates: 21g | Fiber: 0.6g | Sugar: 6.7g | Protein: 3g

Sea Salt and Caramel Pretzel Milkshake

Preparation Time: 2 minutes | Servings: 2

Ingredients:

½ cup whole milk

⅓ pretzels, broken

1½ cups vanilla ice cream

2 tablespoons caramel sauce

2 pinches sea salt

Preparation:

1. Move the ice cream into a CREAMi pint container. 2. Use a spoon to make a hole that is 1½ inches wide in the pint's bottom. 3. Add the remaining ingredients to the hole. 4. Fasten the lid of the pint and freeze for 24 hours. 5. After 24 hours, open the pint, fix it into the outer bowl of Ninja CREAMi along with the 'Creamerizer paddle'. 6. Fasten the lid, turn on the 'Power Button', and select the 'MILKSHAKE' function. 7. Ladle out the shake into serving glasses and serve chilled.

Nutritional Information per Serving:

Calories: 193 | Fat: 7g | Sat Fat: 4g | Carbohydrates: 23g | Fiber: 0.5g | Sugar: 13g | Protein: 4g

Mixed Berries Milkshake

Preparation Time: 10 minutes | Servings: 2

Ingredients:

½ cup milk

½ cup fresh mixed berries

1½ cups vanilla ice cream

Preparation:

1. Move the ice cream, milk, and berries into a CREAMi pint container. 2. Fasten the lid of the pint and freeze for 24 hours. 3. After 24 hours, open the pint, fix it into the outer bowl of Ninja CREAMi along with the 'Creamerizer paddle'. 4. Fasten the lid, turn on the 'Power Button', and select the 'MILKSHAKE' function. 5. Ladle out the shake into serving glasses and serve chilled.

Nutritional Information per Serving:

Calories: 153 | Fat: 6.6g | Sat Fat: 4.1g | Carbohydrates: 19.3g | Fiber: 1.6g | Sugar: 15.8g | Protein: 4g

Cherry Vanilla Milkshake

Preparation Time: 5 minutes | Servings: 2

Ingredients:

3 scoops vanilla ice cream, softened

¼ cup milk, chilled

1 cup cherries, pitted and halved

Preparation:

1. Move all the ingredients into a CREAMi pint container. 2. Fasten the lid of the pint and freeze for 24 hours. 3. After 24 hours, open the pint, fix it into the outer bowl of Ninja CREAMi along with the 'Creamerizer paddle'. 4. Fasten the lid, turn on the 'Power Button', and select the 'MILKSHAKE' function. 5. Ladle out the shake into serving glasses and serve chilled.

Nutritional Information per Serving:

Calories: 130 | Fat: 2g | Sat Fat: 1g | Carbohydrates: 25g | Fiber: 2g | Sugar: 21g | Protein: 3g

Chocolate Yogurt Milkshake

Preparation Time: 10 minutes | Servings: 2

Ingredients:

1 scoop chocolate whey protein powder   1 cup whole milk

1 cup frozen chocolate yogurt

Preparation:

1. Move the yogurt, protein powder, and milk into a CREAMi pint container. 2. Fasten the lid of the pint and freeze for 24 hours. 3. After 24 hours, open the pint, fix it into the outer bowl of Ninja CREAMi along with the 'Creamerizer paddle'. 4. Fasten the lid, turn on the 'Power Button', and select the 'MILKSHAKE' function. 5. Ladle out the shake into serving glasses and serve chilled.

Nutritional Information per Serving:

Calories: 242 | Fat: 4.8g | Sat Fat: 2.8g | Carbohydrates: 30.7g | Fiber: 0.4g | Sugar: 27.5g | Protein: 18.6g

Chapter 4 Ice Creams

Wellness Earl Grey Tea Ice Cream

Preparation Time: 25 minutes | Cooking Time: 25 minutes | Servings: 4

Ingredients:

1 cup whole milk

1 cup heavy cream

5 tablespoons monk fruit sweetener

3 bags of Earl Grey tea

Preparation:

1. In a medium pot, merge the milk and heavy cream. 2. Place the saucepan on the stovetop and cook until steam starts to rise. 3. Fold in the monk fruit sweetener and mix well. 4. Add tea bags, steep for 20 minutes, and then remove. 5. Remove the base from the heat and let it cool. 6. Move the mixture into an empty Ninja CREAMI pint. 7. Fasten the lid of the pint and freeze for 24 hours. 8. After 24 hours, open the pint, fix it into the outer bowl of Ninja CREAMi along with the 'Creamerizer paddle'. 9. Fasten the lid, turn on the 'Power Button', and select the 'ICE CREAM' function. 10. Dish out the ice cream from the pint and serve chilled.

Nutritional Information per Serving:

Calories: 140 | Fat: 13g | Sat Fat: 8g | Carbohydrates: 3.9g | Fiber: 0g | Sugar: 3.2g | Protein: 2g

Sweet Carrot Ice Cream

Preparation Time: 10 minutes | Cooking Time: 20 minutes | Servings: 6

Ingredients:

2 cups heavy cream

½ cup sugar, granulated

¾ teaspoon kosher salt

2 teaspoons apple cider vinegar

2 cups whole milk

⅓ cup light brown sugar

4 carrots, peeled and chopped

Preparation:

1. In a saucepan, merge together the cream, milk, sugars, and salt. 2. Whisk over low heat and stir in the carrots. 3. Cook the carrots until they are tender. 4. Move the mixture into an empty Ninja CREAMI pint after letting it cool down. 5. Merge in the vinegar and salt. 6. Fasten the lid of the pint and freeze for 24 hours. 7. After 24 hours, open the pint, fix it into the outer bowl of Ninja CREAMi along with the 'Creamerizer paddle'. 8. Fasten the lid, turn on the 'Power Button', and select the 'ICE CREAM' function. 9. Dish out the ice cream from the pint and serve chilled.

Nutritional Information per Serving:

Calories: 297 | Fat: 17.4g | Sat Fat: 10.7g | Carbohydrates: 33.4g | Fiber: 1g | Sugar: 30.8g | Protein: 3.8g

Taro Puree Ice Cream

Preparation Time: 15 minutes | Cooking Time: 30 minutes | Servings: 5

Ingredients:

1 cup condensed milk, sweetened

1 cup heavy cream, chilled

½ lb. taro, peeled

Preparation:

1. Boil the taros for 30 minutes until tender, then drain them. 2. Move the boiled taros into an empty Ninja CREAMI pint along with heavy cream and condensed milk. 3. Fasten the lid of the pint and freeze for 24 hours. 4. After 24 hours, open the pint, fix it into the outer bowl of Ninja CREAMi along with the 'Creamerizer paddle'.' 5. Fasten the lid, turn on the 'Power Button', and select the 'ICE CREAM' function. 6. Dish out the ice cream from the pint and serve chilled.

Nutritional Information per Serving:

Calories: 330 | Fat: 14.3g | Sat Fat: 8.9g | Carbohydrates: 46g | Fiber: 1.9g | Sugar: 33.5g | Protein: 6g

Peanut Butter Vanilla Ice Cream

Preparation Time: 10 minutes | Servings: 4

Ingredients:

1¾ cups milk, skimmed

¼ cup stevia-cane sugar blend

3 tablespoons smooth peanut butter

1 teaspoon vanilla extract

Preparation:

1. In a bowl, merge together all the ingredients and thoroughly whisk. 2. Move the mixture into an empty Ninja CREAMI pint. 3. Fasten the lid of the pint and freeze for 24 hours. 4. After 24 hours, open the pint, fix it into the outer bowl of Ninja CREAMi along with the 'Creamerizer paddle'. 5. Fasten the lid, turn on the 'Power Button', and select the 'ICE CREAM' function. 6. Dish out the ice cream from the pint and serve chilled.

Nutritional Information per Serving:

Calories: 143 | Fat: 6.1g | Sat Fat: 1.2g | Carbohydrates: 19.7g | Fiber: 0.7g | Sugar: 18.5g | Protein: 6.5g

Custard Oreo Ice Cream

Preparation Time: 15 minutes | Cooking Time: 10 minutes | Servings: 4

Ingredients:

10 Oreos, roughly chopped

1 cup heavy cream

½ cup sugar

½ cup whole milk

1 teaspoon vanilla extract

3 egg yolks

⅛ teaspoon salt

Preparation:

1. In a saucepan, merge half the sugar with ½ cup of milk and salt. 2. Cook over medium heat until it starts simmering, then eliminate from heat. 3. In a small bowl, merge the egg yolks with sugar and remaining milk. 4. Move this mixture into the saucepan and cook for 5 minutes. 5. Eliminate the pot from heat and set aside to cool it down. 6. Merge in the cream, chopped cookies, and vanilla. 7. Move the mixture into an empty Ninja CREAMI pint. 8. Fasten the lid of the pint and freeze for 24 hours. 9. After 24 hours, open the pint, fix it into the outer bowl of Ninja CREAMi along with the 'Creamerizer paddle'. 10. Fasten the lid, turn on the 'Power Button', and select the 'ICE CREAM' function. 11. Dish out the ice cream from the pint and serve chilled.

Nutritional Information per Serving:

Calories: 2109 | Fat: 105.5g | Sat Fat: 66.2g | Carbohydrates: 257.8g | Fiber: 2.5g | Sugar: 204.3g | Protein: 43.6g

Chocolate Broccoli Ice Cream

Preparation Time: 5 minutes | Servings: 2

Ingredients:

¼ cup sugar

1½ tablespoons cocoa powder

¼ cup frozen broccoli florets, thawed

½ cup whole milk

4 tablespoons heavy cream

Preparation:

1. Blitz broccoli, sugar, milk, and cocoa powder in a blender until smooth. 2. Move the mixture into an empty Ninja CREAMI pint. 3. Fasten the lid of the pint and freeze for 24 hours. 4. After 24 hours, open the pint, fix it into the outer bowl of Ninja CREAMi along with the 'Creamerizer paddle'. 5. Fasten the lid, turn on the 'Power Button', and select the 'ICE CREAM' function. 6. Dish out the ice cream from the pint and serve chilled.

Nutritional Information per Serving:

Calories: 144 | Fat: 5g | Sat Fat: 3g | Carbohydrates: 21g | Fiber: 0.4g | Sugar: 21g | Protein: 2g

Mellowness Walnut Ice Cream

Preparation Time: 10 minutes | Servings: 4

Ingredients:

1 cup whole milk

3 tablespoons walnut paste, smooth

1 tablespoon heavy whipped cream

1 teaspoon vanilla extract

Preparation:

1. In a large bowl, merge together all the ingredients until combined. 2. Move the mixture into an empty Ninja CREAMI pint. 3. Fasten the lid of the pint and freeze for 24 hours. 4. After 24 hours, open the pint, fix it into the outer bowl of Ninja CREAMi along with the 'Creamerizer paddle'. 5. Fasten the lid, turn on the 'Power Button', and select the 'ICE CREAM' function. 6. Dish out the ice cream from the pint and serve chilled.

Nutritional Information per Serving:

Calories: 90 | Fat: 8g | Sat Fat: 3g | Carbohydrates: 8g | Fiber: 0g | Sugar: 5g | Protein: 2g

Canary Pear Ice Cream

Preparation Time: 15 minutes | Cooking Time: 15 minutes | Servings: 4

Ingredients:

1 (14-ounce) can full-fat unsweetened coconut milk

3 medium pears, peeled, cored and cut into

1-inch pieces

½ cup sugar, granulated

Preparation:

1. In a saucepan, merge together all the ingredients and stir well. 2. Thoroughly boil and switch the heat to low, so that it simmers for 10 minutes. 3. Eliminate from the heat and blitz the mixture after it is cooled down. 4. Move the mixture into an empty Ninja CREAMI pint. 5. Fasten the lid of the pint and freeze for 24 hours. 6. After 24 hours, open the pint, fix it into the outer bowl of Ninja CREAMi along with the 'Creamerizer paddle'. 7. Fasten the lid, turn on the 'Power Button', and select the 'ICE CREAM' function. 8. Dish out the ice cream from the pint and serve chilled.

Nutritional Information per Serving:

Calories: 368 | Fat: 18.5g | Sat Fat: 168g | Carbohydrates: 51.9g | Fiber: 4.9g | Sugar: 41.8g | Protein: 2.1g

Crunchy Cracker Ice Cream

Preparation Time: 15 minutes | Cooking Time: 35 minutes | Servings: 6

Ingredients:

½ cup Buncha Crunch

½ teaspoon vanilla extract

1½ cups heavy cream

¼ teaspoon xanthan gum

½ teaspoon salt

½ cup mini chocolate chips

1 tablespoon corn syrup

1½ cups whole milk

8 graham crackers, crushed

½ cup light brown sugar

Preparation:

1. In a bowl, merge the brown sugar with graham crackers, salt, and xanthan gum. 2. In a saucepan, cook the milk, cream, corn syrup, and sugar mixture until all lumps are dissolved. 3. Eliminate the pot from heat and fold in the vanilla extract, chocolate chips, and Buncha Crunch. 4. Move the mixture into an empty Ninja CREAMI pint after refrigerating for 6 hours. 5. Fasten the lid of the pint and freeze for 24 hours. 6. After 24 hours, open the pint, fix it into the outer bowl of Ninja CREAMi along with the 'Creamerizer paddle'. 7. Fasten the lid, turn on the 'Power Button', and select the 'ICE CREAM' function. 8. Dish out the ice cream from the pint and serve chilled.

Nutritional Information per Serving:

Calories: 331 | Fat: 17.3g | Sat Fat: 9.8g | Carbohydrates: 44.1g | Fiber: 4.9g | Sugar: 27.2g | Protein: 4.8g

Aroma Coconut Ice Cream

Preparation Time: 10 minutes | Cooking Time: 10 minutes | Servings: 4

Ingredients:

2 tablespoons coconut, shredded

1 cup full-fat unsweetened coconut milk

2 tablespoon whipped cream

⅓ cup sugar, granulated

Preparation:

1. In a saucepan, merge together all the ingredients and simmer for 10 minutes. 2. Eliminate from heat and blitz the mixture after it is cooled down. 3. Move the mixture into an empty Ninja CREAMI pint. 4. Fasten the lid of the pint and freeze for 24 hours. 5. After 24 hours, open the pint, fix it into the outer bowl of Ninja CREAMi along with the 'Creamerizer paddle'. 6. Fasten the lid, turn on the 'Power Button', and select the 'ICE CREAM' function. 7. Dish out the ice cream from the pint and serve chilled.

Nutritional Information per Serving:

Calories: 231 | Fat: 17g | Sat Fat: 14g | Carbohydrates: 20g | Fiber: 1g | Sugar: 18g | Protein: 1.6g

Ginger Snap and Cinnamon Ice Cream

Preparation Time: 10 minutes | Cooking Time: 5 minutes | Servings: 4

Ingredients:

2 cups oat milk

2 teaspoons ground cinnamon

½ teaspoon ground cloves

⅓ cup brown sugar, packed

1½ teaspoons ground ginger

Preparation:

1. In a small saucepan, merge together all the ingredients and stir well. 2. Cook for 5 minutes and eliminate from the heat. 3. Move the mixture into an empty Ninja CREAMI pint. 4. Fasten the lid of the pint and freeze for 24 hours. 5. After 24 hours, open the pint, fix it into the outer bowl of Ninja CREAMi along with the 'Creamerizer paddle'. 6. Fasten the lid, turn on the 'Power Button', and select the 'ICE CREAM' function. 7. Dish out the ice cream from the pint and serve chilled.

Nutritional Information per Serving:

Calories: 117 | Fat: 1g | Sat Fat: 0g | Carbohydrates: 25g | Fiber: 1.8g | Sugar: 21g | Protein: 2g

Coconut Carrot Cake Ice Cream

Preparation Time: 5 minutes | Cooking Time: 5 minutes | Servings: 4

Ingredients:

½ cup whole milk

¾ cup carrots, shredded

¼ cup brown sugar

¼ cup cream cheese

2 tablespoons shredded coconut

1 cup heavy cream

¼ cup + 1 tablespoon white sugar

⅛ teaspoon cinnamon

1 teaspoon vanilla extract

2 tablespoons toasted walnuts, chopped

2 tablespoons golden raisins, roughly chopped

Preparation:

1. In a saucepan, merge together milk, heavy cream, carrots, cinnamon, and white and brown sugar. 2. Cook for 5 minutes until the carrots are tender. 3. In a bowl, merge together cream cheese and vanilla extract. 4. Fold in the carrots mixture and thoroughly stir. 5. Move the mixture into an empty Ninja CREAMI pint. 6. Fasten the lid of the pint and freeze for 24 hours. 7. After 24 hours, open the pint, fix it into the outer bowl of Ninja CREAMi along with the 'Creamerizer paddle'. 8. Fasten the lid, turn on the 'Power Button', and select the 'ICE CREAM' function. 9. Dish out the ice cream from the pint and serve chilled.

Nutritional Information per Serving:

Calories: 265 | Fat: 20g | Sat Fat: 11g | Carbohydrates: 18g | Fiber: 1.2g | Sugar: 14g | Protein: 4g

Chapter 5 Ice Cream Mix-Ins

Chocolate Nut Ice cream

Preparation Time: 10 minutes | Servings: 6

Ingredients:

1 cup whole milk

⅓ cup sugar, granulated

2 tablespoons cocoa powder

½ cup walnuts, chopped

¾ cup heavy cream

2 tablespoons mini chocolate chips

½ cup brownies, chopped

Preparation:

1. In a blender, blitz all the ingredients except walnuts until smooth. 2. Move the mixture into an empty Ninja CREAMI pint. 3. Fasten the lid of the pint and freeze for 24 hours. 4. After 24 hours, open the pint, fix it into the outer bowl of Ninja CREAMi along with the 'Creamerizer paddle'. 5. Fasten the lid, turn on the 'Power Button', and select the 'ICE CREAM' function. 6. Now, make a wide hole in the center that reaches the bottom of the pint. 7. Put the walnuts in the hole and select the 'MIX-IN' function. 8. Dish out the ice cream from the pint and serve chilled.

Nutritional Information per Serving:

Calories: 269 | Fat: 16.7g | Sat Fat: 5.8g | Carbohydrates: 28.6g | Fiber: 1.3g | Sugar: 13.5g | Protein: 5.4g

Pretzel Cheese Ice Cream

Preparation Time: 10 minutes | Cooking Time: 1 minute | Servings: 2

Ingredients:

½ tablespoon cream cheese, softened

⅓ cup cream

1 tablespoon vanilla extract

Mix-Ins

½ tablespoon mini pretzels

3 tablespoons sugar

½ cup whole milk

Preparation:

1. In a large microwave-safe bowl, microwave the cream cheese for 12 seconds. 2. In a bowl, merge together the sugar and vanilla extract. Let it rest for 30 minutes. 3. Fold in the heavy cream and milk and whisk well. 4. Move the mixture into an empty Ninja CREAMI pint. 5. Fasten the lid of the pint and freeze for 24 hours. 6. After 24 hours, open the pint, fix it into the outer bowl of Ninja CREAMi along with the 'Creamerizer paddle'. 7. Fasten the lid, turn on the 'Power Button', and select the 'ICE CREAM' function. 8. Now, make a wide hole in the center that reaches the bottom of the pint. 9. Put the mini pretzels in the hole and select the 'MIX-IN' function. 10. Dish out the ice cream from the pint and serve chilled.

Nutritional Information per Serving:

Calories: 189 | Fat: 11g | Sat Fat: 6.9g | Carbohydrates: 20g | Fiber: 0g | Sugar: 20g | Protein: 2.7g

Peanut n' Grape Jelly Ice Cream

Preparation Time: 25 minutes | Cooking Time: 3 minutes | Servings: 4

Ingredients:

4 large egg yolks

⅓ cup heavy cream

¼ cup smooth peanut butter

¼ cup honey roasted peanuts, chopped

3 tablespoons sugar, granulated

1 cup whole milk

3 tablespoons grape jelly

Preparation:

1. In a small saucepan, merge together the egg yolks and sugar. 2. Fold in the heavy cream, milk, peanut butter, and grape jelly. 3. Cook till it reaches a temperature of 175°F, stirring constantly. 4. Eliminate from the heat and permit it to cool down. 5. Move the mixture into an empty Ninja CREAMI pint. 6. Fasten the lid of the pint and freeze for 24 hours. 7. After 24 hours, open the pint, fix it into the outer bowl of Ninja CREAMi along with the 'Creamerizer paddle'. 8. Fasten the lid, turn on the 'Power Button', and select the 'ICE CREAM' function. 9. Now, make a wide hole in the center that reaches the bottom of the pint. 10. Put the honey roasted peanuts in the hole and select the 'MIX-IN' function. 11. Dish out the ice cream from the pint and serve chilled.

Nutritional Information per Serving:

Calories: 340 | Fat: 22g | Sat Fat: 7g | Carbohydrates: 26g | Fiber: 1g | Sugar: 20g | Protein: 11g

Lavender Wafer Ice Cream

Preparation Time: 15 minutes | Cooking Time: 10 minutes | Servings: 4

Ingredients:

¾ cup heavy cream

⅛ teaspoon salt

¾ cup whole milk

4 drops purple food coloring

1 tablespoon dried culinary lavender

½ cup condensed milk, sweetened

⅓ cup chocolate wafer cookies, crushed

Preparation:

1. In a saucepan, merge together heavy cream, lavender, and salt. 2. Cook for about 10 minutes, stirring constantly. 3. Eliminate from the heat and strain the cream mixture in a large bowl. 4. Eliminate the lavender leaves and fold in the milk, condensed milk and purple food coloring. 5. Move the mixture into an empty Ninja CREAMI pint. 6. Fasten the lid of the pint and freeze for 24 hours. 7. After 24 hours, open the pint, fix it into the outer bowl of Ninja CREAMi along with the 'Creamerizer paddle'. 8. Fasten the lid, turn on the 'Power Button', and select the 'ICE CREAM' function. 9. Now, make a wide hole in the center that reaches the bottom of the pint. 10. Put the crushed cookies in the hole and select the 'MIX-IN' function. 11. Dish out the ice cream from the pint and serve chilled.

Nutritional Information per Serving:

Calories: 229 | Fat: 13.2g | Sat Fat: 8.1g | Carbohydrates: 23.5g | Fiber: 0g | Sugar: 23.2g | Protein: 5g

Brownie Chocolate Chip Ice Cream

Preparation Time: 15 minutes | Servings: 2

Ingredients:

2 eggs

2 cups heavy cream

¼ cup smooth peanut butter

¾ cup sugar

1 cup whole milk

1 cup mini chocolate chips

¼ cup chocolate chunks

¼ cup brownie pieces

Preparation:

1. In a blender, blitz the eggs, sugar, cream, milk, and peanut butter. 2. Now, fold in the chocolate chips and refrigerate for at least an hour. 3. Move the mixture into an empty Ninja CREAMI pint. 4. Fasten the lid of the pint and freeze for 24 hours. 5. After 24 hours, open the pint, fix it into the outer bowl of Ninja CREAMi along with the 'Creamerizer paddle'. 6. Fasten the lid, turn on the 'Power Button', and select the 'ICE CREAM' function. 7. Now, make a wide hole in the center that reaches the bottom of the pint. 8. Put the chocolate chunks and brownie pieces in the hole and select the 'MIX-IN' function. 9. Dish out the ice cream from the pint and serve chilled.

Nutritional Information per Serving:

Calories: 1071 | Fat: 71.2g | Sat Fat: 35.9g | Carbohydrates: 97.5g | Fiber: 1.9g | Sugar: 88.4g | Protein: 20.5g

Almond Cheese Ice Cream

Preparation Time: 25 minutes | Cooking Time: 1 minute | Servings: 2

Ingredients:

1 tablespoon cream cheese, softened

¾ cup heavy cream

¼ cup almonds, chopped

⅓ cup sugar, granulated

1 teaspoon almond extract

1 cup whole milk

Preparation:

1. In a large microwave-safe bowl, microwave the cream cheese for 12 seconds. 2. In a bowl, merge together the sugar and almond extract and thoroughly whisk. 3. Slowly fold in the heavy cream and milk until completely smooth. 4. Move the mixture into an empty Ninja CREAMI pint. 5. Fasten the lid of the pint and freeze for 24 hours. 6. After 24 hours, open the pint, fix it into the outer bowl of Ninja CREAMi along with the 'Creamerizer paddle'. 7. Fasten the lid, turn on the 'Power Button', and select the 'ICE CREAM' function. 8. Now, make a wide hole in the center that reaches the bottom of the pint. 9. Put the almonds in the hole and select the 'MIX-IN' function. 10. Dish out the ice cream from the pint and serve chilled.

Nutritional Information per Serving:

Calories: 347 | Fat: 22g | Sat Fat: 7g | Carbohydrates: 27g | Fiber: 1.9g | Sugar: 21g | Protein: 11g

Caramel Corn and Butterscotch Ice cream

Preparation Time: 10 minutes | Servings: 6

Ingredients:

½ cup butterscotch pieces, chopped

1 cup whole milk

⅓ cup sugar, granulated

¾ cup caramel corn, roughly chopped

¾ cup heavy cream

Preparation:

1. In a blender, blitz pecans with the remaining ingredients except for butterscotch pieces. 2. Move the mixture into an empty Ninja CREAMI pint. 3. Fasten the lid of the pint and freeze for 24 hours. 4. After 24 hours, open the pint, fix it into the outer bowl of Ninja CREAMi along with the 'Creamerizer paddle'. 5. Fasten the lid, turn on the 'Power Button', and select the 'ICE CREAM' function. 6. Now, make a wide hole in the center that reaches the bottom of the pint. 7. Put the butterscotch pieces in the hole and select the 'MIX-IN' function. 8. Dish out the ice cream from the pint and serve chilled.

Nutritional Information per Serving:

Calories: 185 | Fat: 10.2g | Sat Fat: 6.7g | Carbohydrates: 21g | Fiber: 0g | Sugar: 20.8g | Protein: 2.5g

Marshmallow Almond Ice Cream

Preparation Time: 15 minutes | Servings: 4

Ingredients:

1 cup whole milk

½ cup dark brown sugar

1 teaspoon of chocolate extract

2 tablespoons almonds, sliced

2 tablespoons mini chocolate chips

½ cup frozen cauliflower florets, thawed

3 tablespoons dark cocoa powder

⅓ cup heavy cream

2 tablespoons mini marshmallows

Preparation:

1. In a blender, blitz milk, cauliflower, brown sugar, cocoa powder, and chocolate extract. 2. Fold in the heavy cream and mix well. 3. Move the mixture into an empty Ninja CREAMI pint. 4. Fasten the lid of the pint and freeze for 24 hours. 5. After 24 hours, open the pint, fix it into the outer bowl of Ninja CREAMi along with the 'Creamerizer paddle'. 6. Fasten the lid, turn on the 'Power Button', and select the 'ICE CREAM' function. 7. Now, make a wide hole in the center that reaches the bottom of the pint. 8. Put the almonds, marshmallows, and chocolate chips in the hole and select the 'MIX-IN' function. 9. Dish out the ice cream from the pint and serve chilled.

Nutritional Information per Serving:

Calories: 202 | Fat: 9.3g | Sat Fat: 5g | Carbohydrates: 28.7g | Fiber: 2.1g | Sugar: 24.9g | Protein: 4.2g

Cocoa Mint Ice Cream

Preparation Time: 5 minutes | Servings: 4

Ingredients:

½ cup frozen kale, thawed, squeezed dry   chopped

1 cup whole milk   ½ cup dark brown sugar

3 tablespoons dark cocoa powder   1 teaspoon peppermint extract

8 striped peppermint candies, roughly   ⅓ cup heavy cream

Preparation:

1. In a blender, blitz kale, sugar, milk, extract, and cocoa powder. 2. Move the mixture into an empty Ninja CREAMI pint. 3. Fasten the lid of the pint and freeze for 24 hours. 4. After 24 hours, open the pint, fix it into the outer bowl of Ninja CREAMi along with the 'Creamerizer paddle'. 5. Fasten the lid, turn on the 'Power Button', and select the 'ICE CREAM' function. 6. Now, make a wide hole in the center that reaches the bottom of the pint. 7. Put the chopped peppermint candy pieces in the hole and select the 'MIX-IN' function. 8. Dish out the ice cream from the pint and serve chilled.

Nutritional Information per Serving:

Calories: 148 | Fat: 5g | Sat Fat: 3g | Carbohydrates: 22g | Fiber: 0.3g | Sugar: 20g | Protein: 2g

Conclusion

The Ninja™ CREAMi® is a unique and revolutionary way to make frozen desserts in the comfort and safety of your own home. A unique blend of technology, high-grade materials, and an easy-to-follow user interface create a tool that is both simple to use and extremely efficient. Those who want to impress their dinner guests with gourmet frozen desserts can now do so easily with this amazing device that effortlessly transforms any frozen base into delicious ice cream, sorbet, milkshakes, or more at a touch of a button. This versatile device is sure to become an indispensable part of any kitchen.

It goes without saying that the revolutionary Ninja Creami cookbook is an incredible choice for anyone looking for a boost in their cooking repertoire. Not only does it feature a wide range of imaginative recipes, from ice-creams and sorbets to milkshakes and more, but its unique Ninja Creami twist on classic ingredients brings you something truly special. Moreover, the illustrated guide will have you whipping up chilly treats with ease - perfect for feeding your culinary imagination! Generous servings of creativity, convenience and quality await with Ninja Creami - why not get your hands on the cookbook today and get cooking?

Appendix 1 Measurement Conversion Chart

WEIGHT EQUIVALENTS

US STANDARD	METRIC (APPROXINATE)
1 ounce	28 g
2 ounces	57 g
5 ounces	142 g
10 ounces	284 g
15 ounces	425 g
16 ounces (1 pound)	455 g
1.5pounds	680 g
2pounds	907 g

VOLUME EQUIVALENTS (LIQUID)

US STANDARD	US STANDARD (OUNCES)	METRIC (APPROXIMATE)
2 tablespoons	1 fl.oz	30 mL
¼ cup	2 fl.oz	60 mL
½ cup	4 fl.oz	120 mL
1 cup	8 fl.oz	240 mL
1½ cup	12 fl.oz	355 mL
2 cups or 1 pint	16 fl.oz	475 mL
4 cups or 1 quart	32 fl.oz	1 L
1 gallon	128 fl.oz	4 L

TEMPERATURES EQUIVALENTS

FAHRENHEIT(F)	CELSIUS(C) (APPROXIMATE)
225 °F	107 °C
250 °F	120 °C
275 °F	135 °C
300 °F	150 °C
325 °F	160 °C
350 °F	180 °C
375 °F	190 °C
400 °F	205 °C
425 °F	220 °C
450 °F	235 °C
475 °F	245 °C
500 °F	260 °C

VOLUME EQUIVALENTS (DRY)

US STANDARD	METRIC (APPROXIMATE)
⅛ teaspoon	0.5 mL
¼ teaspoon	1 mL
½ teaspoon	2 mL
¾ teaspoon	4 mL
1 teaspoon	5 mL
1 tablespoon	15 mL
¼ cup	59 mL
½ cup	118 mL
¾ cup	177 mL
1 cup	235 mL
2 cups	475 mL
3 cups	700 mL
4 cups	1 L

Appendix 2 Recipes Index

Made in the USA
Coppell, TX
01 May 2023

16280781R00049